On A Collection Of Birds And Mammals From The Colorado Delta, Lower California

Witmer Stone

In the interest of creating a more extensive selection of rare historical book reprints, we have chosen to reproduce this title even though it may possibly have occasional imperfections such as missing and blurred pages, missing text, poor pictures, markings, dark backgrounds and other reproduction issues beyond our control. Because this work is culturally important, we have made it available as a part of our commitment to protecting, preserving and promoting the world's literature. Thank you for your understanding.

On a Collection of Birds and Mammals from the Colorado Delta, Lower California.

BY

WITMER STONE.

With Field Notes by SAMUEL N. RHOADS.

From the Proceedings of The Academy of Natural Sciences of Philadelphia, September, 1905.

Issued December 6, 1905.

ON A COLLECTION OF BIRDS AND MAMMALS FROM THE COLORADO DELTA, LOWER CALIFORNIA.

BY WITMER STONE.

WITH FIELD NOTES BY SAMUEL N. RHOADS.

Early in 1905 Mr. Samuel N. Rhoads made a trip, in the interests of the Academy of Natural Sciences of Philadelphia, through the northwestern portion of Lower California. The birds and mammals, numbering respectively 258 and 117 specimens, have been submitted to me for identification, and are listed below with such comments as they demand. Mr. Rhoads has added his field notes on various of the species, which enhance greatly the value of the report.

The conditions that prevailed during the expedition were peculiarly unfavorable to collecting of any sort, the rain, cold and high water being almost unprecedented. The accounts of the botanical expeditions sent out later by the New York Botanic Garden over the same route taken by Mr. Rhoads give a good idea of the conditions that prevailed (see *Journ. N. Y. Bot. Garden*, May and June, 1905).

Mr. Rhoads "embarked at Yuma, Arizona, in an open rowboat. February 4, accompanied by Mr. H. E. Wilder, of Riverside, and a guide. They descended the Colorado river as far as the mouth of the Hardy river, which is a slackwater bayou emptying into the Colorado about ten miles above the head of the Gulf of California. The Hardy was reached February 8, after an exchange of guides at the Colony, where they were fortunate to secure the services of Frank Tejano, a Cocopah Indian.

"This stream was then ascended as far as the base of the Cocopah range, reaching Bruce's ranch February 15, Pescadoro Slough on the 18th and Cocopah Major Mountain on the 19th. Several days were spent at the last point and also just above the mouth of the Hardy.

"From camp at the base of the Cocopah Knob, after a stay of nine days, the trip was continued overland to Calexico, on the Californian border, which was reached after five days of the most fatiguing driving and marching through the fresh mud and sloughs of the overflowing Colorado.

"During the entire trip more than half of the whole number of days were rainy, and the total precipitation was stated to have been more than often aggregates in this desert region for a period of years. The temperature was correspondingly low, on the 13th reaching 34° with ice in the coffee-pot, something the guide had never seen before in his lifetime of forty-five years. On these accounts the animal life of the region was at a standstill and the results of field work most discouraging."

In the list which follows Mr. Rhoads' field notes are given in quotation marks.

Ovis canadensis cremnobates Elliot. Lower California Sheep.

Three females, one of which was adult, obtained in the Cocopah Mountains, near camp, February 24; also a weathered skull and other bones of an old male.

"Numerous in the Cocopah range. Said to abound on the arid slopes and valleys lying between this and the San Pedro Martir range."

Sigmodon hispidus eremicus Mearns. Western Desert Cotton Rat.

Nineteen specimens of various ages, from the mouth of the Hardy river, the type locality for this race.

"Abounding in the overflow lands where the tules and reeds were a permanent food supply. Not an upland species, but essentially littoral."

Reithrodontomys longicaudus pallidus Rhoads. Lower California Harvest Mouse.

Six specimens from the mouth of the Hardy river.

"Found only in fine grass on the higher banks—situations, however, which would be temporarily overflowed at highest periods of spring tides and freshets. The Sigmodon was abundant in the same locations."

Neotoma intermedia albigula (Hartley). White-throated Wood Rat.

Five specimens from the mouth of the Hardy seem to be referable to this race.

"The large bush nests of this animal were seen at two or three other points in the delta, including the last camp at Mount Major; here they frequented the rocks also, or possibly this was another species. The habits and homes of this animal on the banks of the Hardy resemble those of the mesquite rats in the vicinity of Corpus Christi, Texas. They subsist largely on the bark and twigs as well as the seeds and pods of the mesquite."

Peromyscus eremicus (Baird). Desert Mouse.

Two forms of white-footed mice were obtained by Mr. Rhoads, and typical examples of each were submitted to Mr. W. H. Osgood, of the U. S. Biological Survey, who has kindly identified them.

The present species was abundant in the Cocopah Mountains, where a series of nineteen specimens was secured. A single female was obtained at the mouth of the Hardy, doubtless carried down in the flood, and four were trapped in the hills near the Mexican boundary, on the Colorado river.

"A rock-loving mountain species, whose habitat touches upon but not invades that of *sonoriensis*."

Peromyscus sonoriensis (Le Conte). Sonora White-footed Mouse.

This was the prevalent form in the low ground, nineteen specimens being obtained at the mouth of the Hardy and five others on the Colorado thirty-five miles below Yuma. Four specimens were also trapped in the Cocopahs with the preceding species.

"Excessively abundant in the bottoms, preventing the capture of other small rodents, etc., by incessantly springing the traps. Without studying its anatomy, I should predict that this species was more nearly related to *gossypinus* of the East than to *leucopus*. I base this view solely on its habitat and manner of life."

Perognathus penicillatus angustirostris Osgood. Slender-nosed Pocket Mouse.

Three specimens from the Cocopahs and one from the Colorado river, near the Mexican boundary. In going over the large series of these mice in the Rhoads collection at the Academy, I find among them three examples of *P. fallax pallidus* Mearns, obtained at Mission Creek, California, by R. B. Herron. These, as their labels show, had been separated in 1895 as a distinct race of *fallax* by Mr. Rhoads, but his name has remained in manuscript and the specimens were afterward referred by him to this species.

Perognathus spinatus Merriam. Spiny Pocket Mouse.

Eleven examples, all from the Cocopah Mountains.

"This and the former named inhabit the desert mountain and plain to the edge of the delta bottoms. Their homes are made by tunnelling at the base of greasewood and other low thickset bushes, as well as among the rocky clefts of the hills where any vegetation has a foothold. The entrances to these burrows remain open. They do not plough underground as *Blarina, Scalops, Thomomys*, etc., but excavate and throw out the dirt largely at the mouth of the burrow, thus raising the vicinity of their bush colonies into slight mounds. Both species may be caught at the same entrance on successive nights. They are closely associated with the kangaroo rats in these colonies. Judging by the lack of specimens on coldest nights, I judge there is a short period of intermittent hibernation in February."

Dipodomys merriami arenivagus Elliot. San Felipe Kangaroo Rat.

Three specimens from the Cocopahs. These seem to be referable to Elliot's race, though whether it is really separable from *simiolus* I am in doubt.

"All three were taken at the mouth of the same sand burrow at the base of Mount Major, near camp. This and a large white species, probably *deserti* Stephens, are said by the guides to abound in the sand plains on the borders of the delta all the way to Calexico. If so, this would indicate a continuous distribution toward the habitat of *simiolus* in the Mojave Desert. I doubt the separability of *arenivagus*."

Lepus arizonæ Allen. Arizona Hare.

One example from the Colorado river, near the Mexican boundary line, and another from New river, twelve miles from Calexico.

"A bottom-land species, not abundant because of the overabundance of coyotes."

Pipistrellus hesperus (Allen). Western Bat.

One obtained in the Cocopah Mountains, February 21, identified by Mr. J. A. G. Rehn. The margins of the interfemoral membrane as well as the inner portion of the wing margin is whitish.

Procyon pallidus Merr. Pallid Raccoon.

A specimen from the mouth of the Hardy river and one from the Colony.

"Coons occur everywhere along the river."

Urocyon littoralis (Baird). Coast Fox.

A skull from nine miles west of Bruce's ranch; also a mummified skeleton from Mount Major which could not be preserved.

Canis estor Merriam? Coyote.

Five skulls and four skins, which seem to be referable to this form; but without topotypes for comparison, it is impossible to satisfactorily identify them. That three species of coyotes occur together in the San Pedro Martir Mountains, as stated by Mr. Elliot, seems to me very unlikely.

"Mr. Wilder, whose experience with coyotes extends over a wide territory in the far West, told me he never heard the like of those which nightly sang and yelled us to sleep in the Colorado delta. They were overabundant and easily trapped."

Tursiops gillii Dall. Gill's Dolphin.

One skull, found on the Hardy river at the base of the Cocopah Mountains, fifty miles above the Gulf.

ADDITIONAL SPECIES OBSERVED.

Odocoileus hemionus eremicus (Mearns). Sonoran Mule Deer. Burro Deer.

"It was probably this race which we found inhabiting the delta on the Californian side. The floods had driven them to the uplands, so they were rarely seen, but their old tracks were abundant. Two specimens were shot by a comrade near the last camp, the horns of which were taken home by Mr. Wilder. On the delta this species ruts in February, the fawns being born in August."

Antilocapra americana mexicana Merr. Mexican Antelope.

"A trip was taken to the base of the mountains, nine miles from Bruce's ranch, for this species, but none were seen. Their old tracks were plentiful. About forty miles south of this point, on the mesas of the San Pedro Martir and Major Cocopahs, they are reported to be abundant."

Castor canadensis frondator Mearns. Arizona Beaver.

"Several are trapped in winter on the lower Colorado. I examined some fresh hides in a trapper's camp above the Colony, and a large number taken on Pescadoro Slough, where they are reported more abundant. They make no dams nor any homes in the banks, but raise large flat piles of brush and mud for their homes back in the densely grown sloughs and ponds of the bottoms."

Felis cougar browni (Merr.). Sonoran Puma?

"None seen. Our guide, Frank Tejano, denied having met with this species, but had seen their tracks. He seemed to be in awe of them and declined to give his experiences. They are rare."

Lynx ruffus peninsularis Thomas. Peninsular Wild Cat?

"One or two seen. Not rare."

Taxidea taxus infusca Thomas? Badger.

"Tracks of badgers were seen, as well as holes stated to belong to them."

Thomomys fulvus nigricans Rhoads? Lower Sonoran Mole Rat.

"A few places indicated the presence of some species of this genus even in the bottom lands. None were captured."

BIRDS.

Podilymbus podiceps (Linn.). Pied-billed Grebe.

One specimen from mouth of Hardy river, February 11.

"Only one seen."

Larus philadelphia (Ord.). Bonaparte's Gull.

One secured at the mouth of the Hardy and one thirty miles below Yuma.

"Very scarce and mostly in a half-starved condition, appearing to suffer greatly from the unusual cold.

Nycticorax n. nævius (Bodd.). Night Heron.

One at "Colony," February 7.

"Without exception the most abundant water bird on the river. Some individuals appeared to belong to the yellow-crowned species."

Symphemia semipalmata inornata Brewst. Western Willet.

One obtained at the mouth of the Hardy.

"The only one noted."

Lophortyx gambelii (Gambel). Gambel's Quail.

A number of specimens from the Cocopah Major Mountains, several from the mouth of the Hardy, and one fifty miles below Yuma.

"They were subsisting almost wholly on the mistletoe berries growing on the mesquites."

Accipiter velox (Wils.). Sharp-shinned Hawk.

One obtained on the Colorado thirty miles below Yuma.

"Rarely seen."

Falco sparverius phalæna (Lesson). Desert Sparrow Hawk.

Specimens obtained on the Hardy river and at Bruce's ranch.

"A scarce bird."

Bubo virginianus pallescens Stone.

One specimen from midway up the Hardy river, and another without locality.

"Found nesting at Bruce's ranch and everywhere abundant."

Centurus uropygialis (Baird). Gila Woodpecker.

Specimens from the Hardy river and Cocopah Major Mountains, as well as on the Colorado near the Mexican boundary. These birds are all typical.

"These also lived largely on the mistletoe berries."

Dryobates scalaris lucasanus (Xantus). Saint Lucas Woodpecker.

Two specimens from Colony and two from the Cocopah Major Mountains. The white on the tail feathers is variable, but less so in the females than in the males. The Colony specimens approach *bairdi*, but the others are *lucasanus*. A specimen in the Academy's collection obtained in June, 1852, by Col. McCall, in southern California, is a marked example of *lucasanus*. After examining a number of these birds, I can see no reason for elevating the Lower Californian race to specific rank, as has recently been done by Mr. William Brewster.

"These birds were extremely wild and difficult to secure."

Calypte costæ (Bourc.). Costa's Hummingbird.

Two specimens from Cocopah Major Mountains.

"These tiny birds were breeding, one of the specimens shot showing bodily marks of protracted incubation on the 21st of February."

Selasphorus rufus (Gmel.). Rufous Hummingbird.

One example from the Cocopahs.

"This bird was going through its aerial love antics in February with all the energy of a midsummer madness. This was the more remarkable as all other bird and animal life was in its deepest winter lethargy during my entire stay at this camp, and the temperature frequently fell to near 45°. This coincides with the actions of *rufus* in the vicinity of Puget Sound, as observed by me in early April, 1903, where I found it breeding though frost frequently formed at night."

Myiarchus cinereus (Lawr.). Ash-throated Flycatcher.

Specimens from Colony and Cocopahs.

"Of uniform but scanty distribution. They nested on the tops of the densely wooded cottonwood and willow bottoms, uttering frequent ejaculations as they darted upward for insects. Generally in quartettes, sometimes five or six within hearing."

Sayornis saya (Bonap.). Say's Phœbe.

One from Bruce's ranch and another from the California-Mexican boundary on the Colorado.

"Wherever we reached bluffs or other elevations not bottom land, this solitaire of the mountains and foothills is wont to appear. Its weird and plaintive cry is in impressive keeping with these barren solitudes."

Sayornis nigricans (Sw.). Black Phœbe.

Obtained at Bruce's ranch, and at the mouth of the Hardy river. The under-tail coverts appear perfectly white, although the longer ones are dusky centrally for more than half their length.

"One of the most lively bits of bird life, which relieved the tedium of our boat journey, was the frequent sight of these birds sitting on the floating drift and hawking flies and other insects from the steaming surface of Colorado of a chilly morning."

Pyrocephalus rubineus mexicanus (Scl.). Vermilion Flycatcher.

Several from the mouth of the Hardy, and also from Pescadoro Slough.

"We were sure to find one or more pairs of these in the mesquite groves. They seem to continue their conjugal attachments all winter, some pairs being inseparable. They furnished the only strong bit of color to be seen in the wintry landscape of the Colorado delta in February. The males on warm days were performing their whimsical little flight songs and tumbling feats, but there was no other sign or suggestion that this had anything to do with sexual excitement."

Corvus corax sinuatus (Wagl.). American Raven.

One obtained at the mouth of the Hardy.

"Numerous everywhere. Some of the ravens may have been the white-necked species. While at Cocopah Major I was entertained by the love antics and really wonderful medley of sounds which a love-sick raven is able to make. Some of these are truly melodious modulations of the so-called 'croak,' and run through quite a slice of the gamut. In addition to this they can tumble, twist, dive, soar and sport about the fleeting form of their mate with all the abandon and daring of less sedate and more elegant masters of the air."

Molothrus ater obscurus (Gmel.). Dwarf Cowbird.

One example taken on the lower Colorado, above Colony.

"They were associated with flocks of Redwings. Some were seen near Pescadoro Slough."

Agelaius phœniceus sonoriensis Ridgw. Sonoran Redwing.

Obtained along the Colorado above Colony, and at the mouth of the Hardy, as well as at Pescadoro Slough. I find it very difficult to separate this form from *neutralis*, and question whether the two will prove distinct when full series representing all seasonal variations are available for comparison. The specimens under consideration might be either form so far as measurements go, but the stripes on the breast of the females appear narrower than in San Diegan birds.

Sturnella magna neglecta (And.). Western Meadow Lark.

Several obtained about the mouth of the Hardy and one farther up the river, all of them typical *neglecta*.

"A rare bird except in open savannas along the Hardy river at two or three points."

Carpodacus mexicanus frontalis (Say). House Finch.

Three specimens taken on the Cocopah Major Mountains.

"Small flocks in the foothills; none seen down the river."

Astragalinus lawrencei (Cass.). Lawrence's Goldfinch.

Three examples from the Cocopahs.

"Two of this, or possibly another Goldfinch, were seen on a mesa above Colony."

Passerculus sandwichensis alaudinus (Bonap.). Western Savanna Sparrow.

A number from the mouth of the Hardy river and from Bruce's ranch. Several of them are in the spring molt.

"This species, with flocks of Brewer's and Chipping Sparrows and Abert's Towhee, were in great numbers in some favorable mesquite bottoms where grass weeds and mistletoe berries formed an abundant harvest."

Passerculus rostratus (Cass.). Large-billed Sparrow.

Five specimens from the mouth of the Hardy, all of them typical *rostratus*.

"These occupied a narrow strip or beach of marsh grass or sedge bordering the river and reaching far back over the mesquite bottom to higher open ground. They kept close to the river bank when flushed, while the Savannas flew across to the upland. About twenty *rostratus* were seen."

Zonotrichia leucophrys gambelii (Nutt.). Intermediate Sparrow.

Obtained at Bruce's ranch and Cocopah Mountains.

Spizella socialis arizonæ Coues. Western Chipping Sparrow.

Specimens from mouth of the Hardy and Bruce's ranch.

Spizella breweri Cass. Brewer's Sparrow.

Found at Bruce's ranch and on the Cocopahs.

Junco hyemalis (Linn.). Slate-colored Junco.

One typical male example from the Cocopah Major Mountains, February 24.

Junco oreganus thurberi Anthony. Thurber's Junco.

Three specimens from the Cocopahs, one of them not typical, but nearer to this than any other form.

Amphispiza bilineata deserticola Ridgw. Desert Sparrow.

One obtained on the Cocopah Mountains.

"Two or three were found in the chapparal, very wary indeed. The males occasionally uttered a sweet song. I saw no others."

Melospiza cinerea fallax (Baird). Desert Song Sparrow.

A number of specimens from the mouth of the Hardy, Bruce's ranch and the Colorado sixty miles below Yuma.

"The song of this form is precisely like that of our Eastern bird, and was a constant reminder of the winter minstrelsy of my home in the Delaware River Valley. They are very abundant in the whole delta."

Pipilo aberti Baird. Abert's Towhee.

Obtained on the Colorado and Hardy rivers at various points, and in the Cocopah Mountains.

"This peculiar or, rather, original bird character is abundant. In habits and appearance and in character also it reminds one of a female cardinal Grosbeak. Its voice or call note completes the illusion. Its song I never heard. That, together with its anatomy, may be sufficient proof that the systematists have not gone wrong in naming it *Pipilo*. No cardinals seem to inhabit its rendezvous in the Colorado delta, and that is another puzzling factor in the life history of Abert's Towhee."

Iridoprocne bicolor (Vieill.). Tree Swallow.

One example from Bruce's ranch.

"Several flocks seen."

Phainopepla nitens (Swains). Phainopepla.

Two examples on the Colorado fifty miles below Yuma and one from the Cocopahs.

"Wherever mesquites and their parasitic berries abounded plenty of these shining crested fellows plaintively flitted about from one high perch to another."

Lanius ludovicianus gambeli Ridgw. California Shrike.

Three specimens from the mouth of the Hardy river come nearer to *gambeli* than any other race, though they are not quite typical.

"Another was taken near Pescadoro Slough and several seen at the Mount Major camp."

Helminthophila celata lutescens (Ridgw.). Lutescent Warbler.

One obtained at Bruce's ranch, February 16.

"No others seen."

Dendroica auduboni (Towns.). Audubon's Warbler.

One from Colony and one from the Colorado river near the Mexican boundary.

"Exceedingly abundant everywhere along our route."

Anthus pensilvanicus (Lath.). American Pipit.

One specimen secured on the Hardy river, February 18.

"A very few seen on the Hardy only."

Toxostoma crissale Henry. Crissal Thrasher.

Two from the Cocopah Mountains.

"About five seen altogether. Occasionally one would sing a little, but they were only beginning. Only found in the foothill chapparal above high-water mark, and very shy and cunning in their terrestrial manœuvres to outwit the man with a gun."

Heleodytes brunneicapillus couesi (Sharpe).

Specimens from various points along the Hardy river from its mouth to the Cocopah Mountains.

"Frequenting both the arid foothills and the mesquite bottoms."

Salpinctes obsoletus (Say). Rock Wren.

Six specimens from the Cocopahs and one from the Colorado river near the Mexican boundary in southeastern California.

"A wonderful member of a wonderful family. Its life history, who can tell it? Sprite, sylph, orpheus of the barren mountains, what man could put thy likeness on paper or reveal to the reader thy inmost life? Now that the quest is over and I see seven skins lying side by side in the tray named and numbered, I trow they will be the last of that happy family to serve the demands of science."

Troglodytes aedon parkmanii (Aud.). Parkman's Wren.

One from Bruce's ranch. I follow Mr. Ridgway in uniting *parkmanii* and *aztecus*.

"A few, two or three, were seen at Mount Major."

Telmatodytes palustris paludicola (Baird). Tulé Wren.

Two specimens obtained at the mouth of the Hardy.

"They were numerous near our first camp on the Hardy, keeping close to the tules along the river bank. Very few seen farther up."

Telmatodytes palustris plesius (Oberholser). Western Marsh Wren.

One example of this race, associated with the above.

"No others noted."

Auriparus flaviceps (Sund.). Verdin.

Specimens from the mouth of the Hardy, Bruce's ranch and the Cocopahs.

"Uniformly distributed in the mesquite. One was caught in its gourd-like roosting nest. It sat with its tail projecting from the opening, so as to void all excrement on the ground during the night and keep its winter quarters cleanly."

Regulus calendula (Linn.). Ruby-crowned Kinglet.

One specimen.

"Many seen on both streams."

Polioptila cærulea obscura Ridgw. Western Gnatcatcher.

One from the Mexican boundary and one from Bruce's ranch.

"Abundant and always making a fuss out of proportion to its size."

Polioptila plumbea Baird. Plumbeous Gnatcatcher.

Specimens from Bruce's ranch, Pescadoro Slough and the Cocopah Mountains.

Mimus polyglottos leucopterus (Vigors). Western Mockingbird.

Three examples from the Cocopahs.

"I do not remember seeing any other specimens than those noted at our Mount Major camp. They were beginning to sing."

ADDITIONAL SPECIES OBSERVED BY MR. RHOADS.

Larus occidentalis Aud. Western Gull.

Very abundant on the Colorado and its tributaries.

Larus argentatus Linn. Herring Gull.

A few seen on both the Colorado and the Hardy.

Larus californicus Lawr. California Gull.

A few seen.

Larus heermanni Cass. Heermann's Gull.

A few seen as far up as Yuma, Arizona.

Sterna elegans Gambel?

A few terns were seen in pairs on all the waters visited, either *S. elegans* or *S. dougalli* or both.

Sterna antillarum (Less.)? Least Tern.

Three or four very small terns were probably this species.

Phalacrocorax mexicanus (Brandt). Mexican Cormorant.

Exceedingly abundant, fishing in great shoals with the pelicans.

Pelecanus erythrorhynchos Gmel. American White Pelican.

"Increasingly abundant as Yuma disappeared in our wake, these splendid lordly birds were an ever-present source of delight and admiration during the remainder of our journey. At our camp on the upper Hardy at Mount Major, they came regularly every morning to fish in a lagoon formed by the recent floods directly in front of the camp. Sometimes there would be half a thousand of them, with hundreds of Cormorants plunging about at once. On the outskirts of the fray Great White Egrets gathered the fragments of this royal feast.

Merganser americanus (Cass.). American Merganser.

A few.

Merganser serrator (Linn.). Red-breasted Merganser.
Many.

Anas boschas Linn. Mallard.
Abundant.

Nettion carolinensis Gmel. Green-winged Teal.
Several flocks.

Spatula clypeata (Linn.). Shoveller.
Several.

Dafila acuta (Linn.). Pintail.
Several.

Erismatura jamaicensis (Gmel.). Ruddy Duck.

Chen hyperborea (Pall.). Lesser Snow Goose.
In great flocks going northward over the Cocopah Major, also near the mouth of the Hardy.

Branta canadensis subsp.?
A form of this species was continually going toward the coast from the delta, mostly at great elevations.

Tantalus loculator Linn.? Wood Ibis.
A few seen.

Ardea herodias Linn. Great Blue Heron.
Very abundant.

Egretta candidissima (Gmel.). Snowy Heron.
Several seen up the Hardy, especially at the Mount Major camp.

Grus mexicana (Müll.). Sandhill Crane.
Abundant.

Tringa minutilla Vieill. Least Sandpiper.
A few seen.

Actitis macularia (Linn.). Spotted Sandpiper.
Often seen.

Numenius hudsonicus Lath. Hudsonian Curlew.
Two flocks on the Hardy.

Oxyechus vociferus (Linn.). Killdeer.
Several.

Zenaidura macroura (Linn.). Mourning Dove.
Two or three seen near Colony and one or two up the Hardy. Very scarce.

Scardafella inca (Less.). Inca Dove.
A very few seen in the upper Hardy river region.

Pseudogryphus californianus Shaw. California Vulture
One seen at Mount Major camp.

Cathartes aura (Linn.). Turkey Vulture.
Abundant.

Elanus leucurus (Vieill.). White-tailed Kite.
Seen twice along the Hardy.

Circus hudsonius (Linn.). Marsh Hawk.
Frequent.

Accipiter cooperi (Bonap.). Cooper's Hawk.
Several noted

Parabuteo unicinctus harrissi (Aud.). Harris's Hawk.
Numerous.

Buteo borealis calurus (Cass.). Western Redtail.
Abundant.

Buteo lineatus elegans (Cass.) Red-bellied Hawk.
Several.

Buteo swainsoni Bonap. Swainson's Hawk.
Several.

Buteo platypterus (Vieill.). Broad-winged Hawk.
Two or three seen.

Aquila chrysaëtos (Linn.). Golden Eagle.
At Mount Major.

Haliæetus leucocephalus (Linn.). Bald Eagle.
One seen twice, or else two individuals, on the upper Hardy river. Stated to be very rare by our Indian guide.

Polyborus cheriway (Jacq.). Caracara.
Only two seen on the upper Hardy.

Pandion haliaëtus carolinensis (Gmel.). Osprey.
Seen only at Mount Major.

Strix pratincola Bonap. Barn Owl.
One seen above the Colony.

Asio accipitrinus (Pall.). Short-eared Owl.
A few seen near the mouth of the Hardy.

Megascops asio cineraceus Ridgw. Mexican Screech Owl.
Heard several times.

Geococcyx californianus (Less.). Road Runner.

Often seen on the banks of the river.

Ceryle alcyon (Linn.). Belted Kingfisher.

Often seen.

Chordeiles sp.

Two or three seen.

Contopus richardsonii (Swains.). Western Wood Pewee.

Otocoris alpestris pallida Dwight? Sonoran Horned Lark.

A few seen flying overhead.

Corvus sp.

Crows of some species were seen, but rarely.

Euphagus cyanocephalus (Wagl.). Brewer's Blackbird.

Always abundant near human habitations.

Tachycineta thalassina (Swains.). Violet-green Swallow.

Of large flocks seen some seemed to be this species.

Riparia riparia (Linn.). Bank Swallow.

Several seen along the Hardy river.

Ampelis cedrorum (Vieill.). Cedar Waxwing.

Not many seen.

Galeoscoptes carolinensis (Linn.). Catbird.

I feel sure that this bird was seen and heard two or three times along the Hardy river.

Troglodytes hiemalis pacificus Baird? Western Winter Wren.

Two or three Wrens seen in woods near Colony were presumably this form.

Merula migratoria propinqua Ridgw. Western Robin.

Seen here and there, sometimes numerously.

Sialia mexicana subsp.? Bluebird.

Numerous.

Printed by Libri Plureos GmbH in Hamburg, Germany